Dante Rossetti

THE LIFE AND WORKS OF

Dante Rossetti

ROSSETTI

Richard O'Neill

A Compilation of Works from the
BRIDGEMAN ART LIBRARY

PARRAGON

Box is
non-printing
keyline

This edition first published in 1996 by
Parragon Book Service Ltd
Units 13-17 Avonbridge Industrial Estate
Atlantic Road, Avonmouth, Bristol BS11 9QD

ISBN 0 75251 695 7

Printed in Italy

Editors: Barbara Horn, Alexa Stace, Alison Stace, Tucker Slingsby Ltd and
Jennifer Warner.
Designers: Robert Mathias and Helen Mathias
Picture Research: Kathy Lockley

The publishers would like to thank Joanna Hartley at the
Bridgeman Art Library for her invaluable help.

Dante Gabriel Rossetti 1828 - 1882

IF ANY MAN was born to be a romantic idealist, to excel in both painting and poetry in a manner equalled in Britain only by William Blake, it was Dante Gabriel Rossetti. His parents were the exiled Italian revolutionary and scholar Gabriele Rossetti (1783-1854) and the half Italian Frances Mary Lavinia Rossetti (1800-86), sister of Lord Byron's friend and physician (and reputedly the co-author of *Frankenstein*) John Polidori. His brother, William Michael Rossetti (1829-1919), was a respected scholar and art critic; his younger sister, Christina Rossetti (1830-94), was one of the most remarkable poets of her time.

Although poetry was his first love, Rossetti decided as early as 1841 on an artistic career. His formal studies, first at Cary's Academy (1842-46), then at the Royal Academy Antique School, revealed both major strengths and weaknesses. His imagination, like that of his youthful idol William Blake, was boundless, his handling of colour assured, his draughtsmanship (when he took the trouble) excellent, but he lacked patience. Throughout his life there would be times when he seemed content to let inspiration compensate for faults in such basic skills as perspective.

Seeking a master, Rossetti approached 27-year-old Ford Madox Brown, whose clean line, bold colours and romantic and medieval themes were inspired by the Nazarenes, German artists working in Italy. Soon he was sharing a studio with another young idealist, Holman Hunt. Artists with similar enthusiasms joined their circle, and in September 1848, Rossetti, Hunt, John Everett Millais, William Rossetti, James Collinson, Thomas Woolner and Frederick Stephens formed a 'secret society', the Pre-Raphaelite Brotherhood (PRB). The PRB's ideology, expressed in its short-lived periodical, *The Germ* (1850), was based primarily on the doctrines of the critic John Ruskin. Other influences included an interest in medievalism inspired by the architects of the Gothic Revival and a growing appreciation of Italian 'primitive' art, as well as Nazarene influence through Madox Brown. The PRB aimed to produce works with both aesthetic and moral values in a manner based on the 'purity' and 'simplicity' of the Italian masters predating Raphael(1483-1520).

Rossetti's *Girlhood of Mary Virgin* (page 11) was the first painting shown with the initials 'PRB', in March 1849. Although it was praised, the 'revolutionary' PRB soon attracted severe criticism. So intemperate were some attacks that Rossetti vowed never to exhibit in public again and rarely broke this promise. By *c.*1853 the PRB had dispersed, although a similar group formed around Rossetti, Edward Burne-Jones and William Morris in the late 1850s. Of its original members, only Holman Hunt strove doggedly to remain true to its stated aims.

'Truth to nature' and 'moral seriousness' did not fit well with Rossetti's essential Romanticism. Although he was deeply versed in medieval culture – his translations from Dante remain among the best – his 'Arthurian' pictures, for example, owe more to the nineteenth-century poet Alfred Lord Tennyson than to Chrétien de Troyes, the twelfth-century French author of courtly romances, despite his careful research among illustrated manuscripts. His religious subjects are informed by his own semi-agnostic mysticism, his love of symbol and ritual (he described himself as an 'Art Catholic'), rather than by any moral code.

From around the mid-1850s, Rossetti virtually abandoned oil in favour of watercolour, finding a ready market among a comparatively small circle of patrons. He was a surprisingly good businessman, and by *c.*1860 reckoned to earn some £3,000 (now perhaps £100,000) per year from his art. With his friends Charles Swinburne and James Whistler, he was seen as an arbiter of *avant garde* culture, a pioneer of the 'art for art's sake' movement that would find its fullest expression in the 1890s. His long-lasting (1861-75) association with William Morris and Burne-Jones in 'The Firm', a group of artist-craftsmen who profoundly influenced the decorative arts, saw him execute distinguished work, especially in stained glass.

Rossetti had a dual nature – both aesthete and sensualist. The painter of *Beata Beatrix* (page 39), the sensitive poet, also delighted in pornography. He drew a clear line between spiritual and sexual love. He worshipped his model Elizabeth Siddal, seeing her as Beatrice to his Dante, and may have lived with her in a platonic relationship for several years before their marriage in 1860 – while at the same time pursuing affairs with other models and making regular visits to brothels. After her death in 1862, he transferred his spiritual affections to William Morris's wife Jane. This pure and possibly unconsummated love affair was carried on while he gave orgiastic entertainments at his house in Cheyne Walk, Chelsea in south-west London, and became increasingly enslaved to whisky and the drug chloral. In his last years he was a semi-recluse, dying partially paralyzed after a stroke at the age of 53.

In about 1859 Rossetti had entered a 'Venetian' period, painting a series of female head and shoulders portraits, usually on an intimate scale, in a manner that is reminiscent of Titian or Veronese. His later, larger oils show a coarsening of this style in portrayals of lovely women ('stunners'), often star-crossed lovers of mythology or literature, that blend aesthetic sensibility with raw sexuality. The 'Decadents' and Symbolists of the *fin de siècle* were much influenced by these works, while such eminent critics as Anthony Blunt and Phoebe Pool have traced Rossetti's influence, by way of Art Nouveau and the influential journal *The Studio*, on the young Picasso.

▷ **The Sun May Shine and We Be Cold** 1848

Pen and ink

ROSSETTI'S INTELLECTUAL power and poetic imagination informed his art from the beginning. His earliest graphic works were drawings inspired by his current literary enthusiasms, notably the works of Edgar Allan Poe and Goethe's *Faust*. The literary inspiration for this drawing remains obscure, but the girl's pose, the window-seat and window closely resemble those shown in *The Sleeper*, taken from Poe, while the same image of the Madonna appears in *Faust: Margaret in the Church*, drawings of 1846-47 and 1848 respectively. The drawing dates from the crucial period of Rossetti's early life, when, disillusioned by the academic doctrine of the Royal Academy Antique School, he worked briefly under Ford Madox Brown and then took a studio with Holman Hunt, a co-founder of the Pre-Raphaelite Brotherhood in September 1848. It is inscribed to Alexander Munro, to whom Rossetti first revealed the meaning of the letters 'PRB'.

Detail

▷ The Girlhood of Mary Virgin 1848-49

Oil on canvas

ROSSETTI'S FIRST MAJOR WORK, exhibited at the Hyde Park Corner Gallery, London, March 1849, was also the first shown with the initials 'PRB'. It was executed under the tutelage of Holman Hunt, who later said Rossetti 'howled profanities' at the difficulties encountered, especially with perspective. Yet faults in technique add to the work's *Quattrocento* appeal. Saint Anne, modelled on Rossetti's mother, schools the Blessed Virgin, modelled on Christina Rossetti, in embroidery. Saint Joachim tends a grapevine, source of Eucharistic wine and thus a symbol of Christ's sacrifice, as are the red robe beneath the cruciform trellis and the thorn branch and palms in the foreground. The angel displays a lily, symbol of purity; the books embody such virtues as temperance, faith and fortitude. A dove represents the Holy Ghost. Rossetti was obviously more concerned with symbolic meaning than with religious feeling: the work's original frame bore a sonnet explaining its iconography.

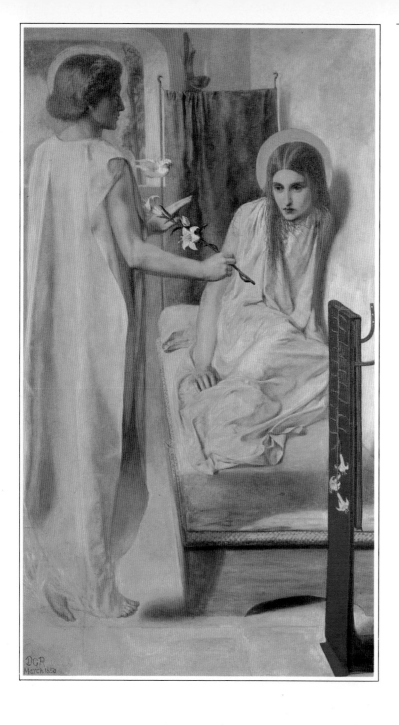

◁ **'Ecce Ancilla Domini!'**
(The Annunciation) 1850

Oil on canvas,
mounted on panel

THIS IS ROSSETTI'S purest
Pre-Raphaelite painting, executed
on a white ground (Holman
Hunt advocated 'wet white' and
a white porcelain palette) with
watercolour brushes, in dry, thin
primary colours. The Virgin
(Christina), in white rather than
traditional blue, is an ordinary
girl – albeit a Pre-Raphaelite
type with fine eyes and enticing
mouth – afraid of the mighty
task forced upon her. Faults in
perspective, such as the blending
of floor and wall; the 'tilted'
bed, and awkward passages,
such as Gabriel's fiery ankles,
are outweighed by the beauty
of the Virgin. *The Girlhood of
Mary Virgin* had been praised,
and sold for 80 guineas (£84;
now *c.* £3,000), but with it Rossetti
had blown the PRB's cover,
exposing its members to academic
fire. They were accused of near
obscene realism (notably in
Dickens' famous attack on
Millais), of wilfully scorning
the great Renaissance masters,
and mocked as painters of
'saints squeezed out perfectly
flat'. Disgusted, Rossetti rarely
exhibited in public again.

**To Caper Nimbly in a Lady's Chamber
to the Lascivious Pleasing of a Lute** 1850

Pen and ink drawing

▷ *Overleaf page 14*

The Borgia Family 1863

Watercolour on paper

▷ *Overleaf page 15*

THE FAILURE OF HIS *Annunciation* to sell (although it did so in 1853) and attacks on the PRB's 'realistic' treatment of scriptural subjects probably caused Rossetti to drop a plan for a *Death of the Virgin* to complete a religious triptych. In common with other members of the Brotherhood, he sought more secular themes. The drawing's caption is taken from Shakespeare's *Richard III* (Act I, Scene 1), although the scene has no bearing on the action of that play.

In 1851 Rossetti began to work it up into a more dramatic composition, appealing to his romantic view of history. In the watercolour (completed in 1859; a version dated 1863 is shown here) the young girl with the lute and her mildly sinister attendants are replaced by members of the Borgia family. The innocent children dance to the music of Lucrezia Borgia (1480-1519) regarded, at least in Rossetti's time, as an infamous poisoner. She is attended by her evil father, Pope Alexander VI, and reputedly homicidal and incestuous brother Cesare. She was modelled by Fanny Cornforth. The striking effect achieved by Rossetti's watercolour technique is especially apparent in Lucrezia's magnificent gown. Its style and pattern were carefully researched. Although Rossetti did not follow Holman Hunt in agonizing over exactitude in every detail, he studied medieval illustrations in the British Museum and elsewhere, and had the run of the excellent collections of Ruskin and his associates.

Dante Rossetti
1850

"To caper nimbly in a lady's chamber
To the lascivious pleasing of a lute."

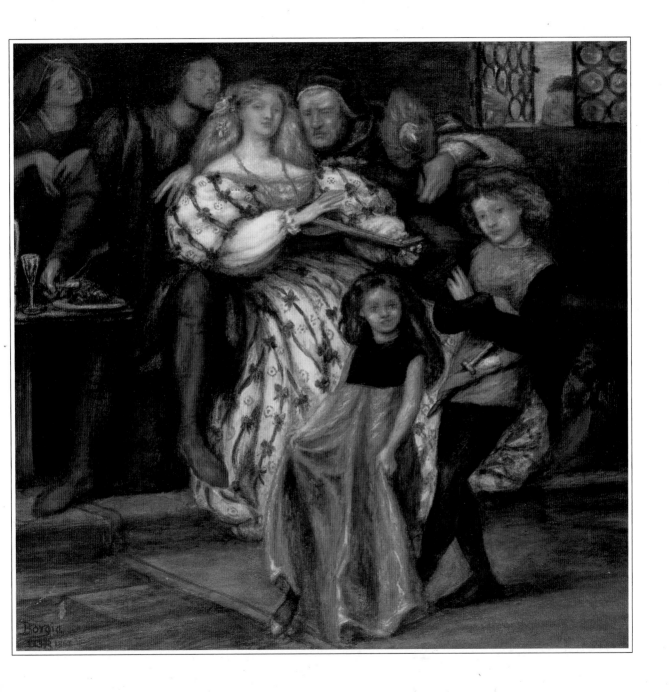

▷ **The Meeting of Dante and Beatrice in Paradise** 1853-54

Watercolour on paper

ROSSETTI'S FATHER was an authority on Dante Alighieri (1265-1321), after whom he named his elder son. His elder daughter, the Anglican nun Maria Francesca Rossetti (1827-76), also wrote scholarly works on the poet. Although Dante Gabriel was often to use Dante's pure love for Beatrice Portinari (d.1290), whom he immortalized in his *Vita Nuova and Divina Commedia,* as both a poetic and artistic metaphor for his own relationship with Elizabeth Siddal, his preoccupation with the medieval Italian poet predated their meeting. His excellent English translations from Dante, although not published until 1861, were accomplished in 1846-50, while among his earliest artistic enthusiasms was that for William Blake, illustrator of the *Divine Comedy.* The watercolour seen here is based on a pen-and-ink drawing of 1849-50, *The Salutation of Beatrice,* a double composition showing first Dante's meeting with Beatrice on Earth and then their encounter in Paradise, where his beloved is accompanied by female saints playing psalteries of the kind often shown in medieval paintings.

Unfinished version

▷ **Found** 1854-81

ROSSETTI'S ONLY 'modern moral subject' was perhaps partly inspired by his own poem *Jenny* (1846) – and partly by his frequent visits to prostitutes, both as a customer and, some biographers say, a 'rescuer'. A young yeoman bringing his calf to market recognizes his former sweetheart (Fanny Cornforth was the model) as a distressed prostitute. He tries to raise her up, but she turns her face to the wall in shame. The painting gave Rossetti endless trouble. The calf '...kicks and fights all the time...punctually attempts suicide by hanging himself...'. It and the brick wall were painted outdoors from life, but Rossetti found it almost impossible to integrate the composition in the studio. Madox Brown noted that he made 'endless emendations, no perceptible progress' – and further complained that while doing so in Brown's chilly studio he wore 'my great coat, which I want, and a pair of my breeches...and the snow comes on!' The work was more than once abandoned and taken up again; final touches were added by Burne-Jones after Rossetti's death.

▷ **Arthur's Tomb** 1854

Watercolour

DURING THE 1850s, annoyed by the criticism levelled at his early oils and probably discouraged by his struggles with *Found*, Rossetti worked increasingly in watercolour, usually on a small scale. His inspiration came largely from illuminated manuscripts of the Middle Ages. Their literary quality appealed to him and their often crowded, elaborate composition, clear, bright colours and disregard for conventional perspective fitted well with his own predilections. *Arthur's Tomb* was among the first of many similar works. Sir Lancelot and Queen Guinevere, the latter in mourning and expressing repentance for her adultery, meet for the last time over the tomb of the king their love has wronged. Here, Rossetti, who had earlier used watercolour techniques in oil painting, achieved a jewel-like effect well suited to his medieval subject by building up layers of colour with an almost dry brush. Thus, while his earlier oils look like watercolours, his watercolours often have the richness of oil paintings.

▷ **The Seed of David**
(side panels) *c.*1856

Watercolour

ONE OF ROSSETTI'S most important
commissions came in March
1856, when Ruskin introduced
him to the architect John Seddon
(1827-1906), the restorer of
Llandaff Cathedral, Cardiff,
Wales. It resulted in what is
possibly his best oil painting,
the large (229 x 152cm; 90 x 60in
centre panel; 185 x 62cm; 73 x
24.5in side panels) altarpiece,
The Seed of David (1858-64).
Rossetti prepared intensively
for the task, even attending
life-drawing classes at Ruskin's
insistence. His major preliminary
work was a much smaller
watercolour, of which the side
panels – the left showing David
the Shepherd; the right David
the King (modelled by William
Morris) – are seen here. The
central panel of the triptych
shows Shepherd and King
worshipping the infant Christ in
the arms of the Virgin (modelled
by Jane Morris). This watercolour
study displays the familiar
faults – flatness of composition
and stiffness of pose – of
Rossetti's medieval period.
The Llandaff altarpiece itself
is a far more richly coloured,
dramatic and successful work.

◁ **The Blue Closet** 1856-57

Watercolour on paper

LIKE A NUMBER OF ROSSETTI'S other medieval exercises, this watercolour has no subject other than itself. It is not grounded in any legend or historical incident. According to his fellow Pre-Raphaelite Frederick Stephens, the artist here aimed 'to symbolize the association of colour with music'. Thus, the work's bright scarlet and green express the sharp sound of the bell, the softer crimson, purple and white echo the tones of the clavichord and lute, while the blue tiles that give the work its name reflect the soft voices of the female musicians. Such exercises in 'colour harmony' bring to mind the paintings of Rossetti's contemporary and friend James McNeill Whistler (1834-1903) and, like those far more unconventional works, they would come to be seen as precursors of the 'art for art's sake' doctrine of the Aesthetic movement.

Elizabeth Siddal 1860

Pencil on paper

◁ *Previous page 25*

'YOU FELLOWS CAN'T TELL what a stupendously beautiful creature I have found!' Thus, late in 1849, the PRB's associate Walter Deverell (1827-54) announced to Hunt and Rossetti his discovery of Elizabeth Siddal (1829-62), an assistant in a London milliner's shop. She became a Pre-Raphaelite icon, modelling for Deverell, Hunt and Millais.

Long immersion in a bath of tepid water as model for Millais' *Ophelia* (1851-52) is said to have contributed to the tuberculosis that increasingly enfeebled her. She first sat for Rossetti in 1851, and within a year was living with him. It has been claimed, however, that their relationship was not sexually consummated until their marriage in 1860, the year of

this charming and gentle drawing. Rossetti was obsessed by an idealized vision of his 'Guggums'. Sexual pleasure he could find with other women, but only Elizabeth could inspire his purest works. Under his teaching she herself became a talented artist (Ruskin ranked her as a genius alongside Rossetti) and an accomplished poet.

▷ **Saint Catherine** 1857

Oil on canvas

THE ONLY OIL of Rossetti's medieval period in the 1850s was commissioned by Ruskin – who disliked the finished work and denounced his friend as 'a conceited monkey, thinking your pictures right when I tell you positively they are wrong!' Although Rossetti carefully researched the costumes of the saint, with her emblems of martyrdom, and the artist who records her

progress, the painting has more to do with his own private symbolism than with Pre-Raphaelite 'truth'. The saint is Elizabeth Siddal, the artist stands for Rossetti; the whole is an expression of their relationship (see also *How They Met Themselves*; page 38). The year of this painting saw the last true PRB project, when Rossetti, Morris, Burne-Jones and

other artists set out to decorate the new Oxford Union with frescoes of ten scenes from Malory's *Morte d'Arthur*. Although the poet Coventry Patmore described the murals as 'so brilliant as to make the walls look like the margin of an illuminated manuscript', the artists' slap-dash technique and the fumes of gas lighting led to their works' decay.

◁ **The Heart of the Night ('Mariana in the South')** 1862

TENNYSON'S POETRY on medieval and Arthurian themes often inspired the Pre-Raphaelites, and in 1855 Rossetti, Millais and Hunt were among artists commisioned to illustrate a new edition of the Laureate's *Poems* (1842). Rossetti lamented that Elizabeth Siddal, many of whose works were illustrations to Tennyson, was not also commissioned. In retaliation, he pushed up the price of his designs and delayed their completion until 1857. His five illustrations included one for *Mariana in the South*, seen here in a later version probably made at the request of a patron – Rossetti did many such copies. Mariana, the deserted lady of Shakespeare's *Measure for Measure*, kneels in an attitude of prayer as she clasps her lover's letters. The right background is taken directly from Dürer's woodcut *Birth of the Virgin* (*c.*1502). It has been suggested that Rossetti, annoyed by Ruskin's unfavourable comparison of all other artists' draughtsmanship with that of Dürer, made this copy to show that he could emulate the

▷ **The Tune of the Seven Towers** 1857

Watercolour on paper

LIKE *The Blue Closet* (page 24), this example of what Rossetti called 'chivalrous Froissartian themes' has a somewhat obscure theme. The air played by the pensive musician, modelled by Elizabeth Siddal, appears to give little pleasure to her brooding, even sinister listeners, while in the background a sorrowful attendant places what may be a symbol of blighted love on the marital bed. It may be that the scallop shell, emblem of the pilgrim, at the musician's throat is another expression of Rossetti's fear of a premature end to the life's journey of his lover. If one disregards the period charm and satisfying colour of the work, then a weakness of this kind of 'fancy picture' becomes apparent. If it is not carried through with complete conviction – as in, for example, *Saint George and Princess Sabra* (page 29) – it tends to become the equivalent of the inferior kind of historical novel, overcrowded with period detail and what Robert Louis Stevenson memorably characterized as 'tushery'.

The Wedding of Saint George and Princess Sabra 1857

Watercolour on canvas

◁ *Previous page 29*

ROSSETTI TOOK THE SUBJECT of what is, perhaps, his finest watercolour and, certainly, his most successful composition in medieval style, from a traditional English ballad. His enduring disdain for conventions of space and perspective – perhaps originally engendered by his enthusiasm for William Blake – proved a virtue in compositions of this kind. The crowding of many elements into a shallow space and the subjection of realism to decorative patterning, produce a striking effect reminiscent of the Books of Hours and Psalters from which Rossetti drew such features as the musical bells played by the musicians flanking the white marriage bed. The Princess Sabra, modelled by 19-year-old Jane Burden, cuts off one of her dark, luxuriant locks for Saint George (probably modelled by William Morris, whom Jane Burden would marry in April 1859). The near heraldic head of the newly-killed dragon, which the warrior saint has apparently brought with him in a packing case, adds an endearingly literal touch to the romantic subject.

Detail

▷ **Mary Magdalene at the Door of Simon the Pharisee** 1858

Pen and Indian ink on paper; mounted on canvas

THE ARTIST'S MOST PAINSTAKING draughtsmanship is admirably displayed in this drawing, which may be intended as an 'antidote' to the troublesome *Found* (page 19). Unlike that work's fallen woman, who turns from her would-be rescuer, the Magdalene is suddenly no longer a part of the throng of courtesans and gallants, no longer hears the musicians, as she becomes aware of the still figure of Christ. However, the picture must be judged as a number of parts, albeit fine ones, that do not constitute a whole, for the eye cannot move easily through it. Perhaps such compartmentalization was the result of Rossetti's ear exposure to Holman Hunt's ideal of purity achieved through painting on a 'wet white' ground, limiting the artist to working on a single passage, that cannot be retouched, at a time. As the critic Quentin Bell observed, this tended to produce a cloisonné effect. The head of Christ was modelled by Burne-Jones, whose drawing *The Wise and Foolish Virgins* (1859) shows the influence of this work.

◁ **Writing on the Sand** 1859

Watercolour on paper

SOME TIME BEFORE the execution of this watercolour, Ruskin had advised Rossetti: 'I think your drawings worth *twenty* times what you ask...yet you must consider market value...and a painful and sad-coloured subject never fetches so much as a pleasant and gay one'. Taken at face value, this charming picture of lovers on a beach seems to show that the artist had decided to take Ruskin's advice. But there may be a sub-text. The lover traces his beloved's portrait (as Rossetti so often portrayed Elizabeth Siddal) in the inconstant sand, where the oncoming waves will soon obliterate it. It has been suggested that this work shows that Rossetti was considering a separation from his ailing lover of some nine years' standing. In fact, although he continued his affair with Fanny Cornforth, his casual infidelities with others and his visits to prostitutes, he did not do so. Elizabeth's health continued to deteriorate, but in May 1860 she and Rossetti were married.

Dantis Amor 1860

Oil on panel

◁ *Previous page 35*

HERE, THE FLAT, DECORATIVE
elements in Rossetti's work
appear to have taken over
completely. The explanation
lies in the panel's original
purpose, as part of the scheme
of decoration for an early
piece of furniture by William
Morris. This was a 'medieval'
settle (high-backed bench)
designed around 1856, when
Morris and Burne-Jones
worked with Rossetti in Red
Lion Square, London. It was
built by a local carpenter and
beautified by Rossetti and
Morris with scenes from
Dante and Malory. A caricature
by Max Beerbohm shows
'Topsy' (the burly Morris)
and 'Ned' (the etiolated
Burne-Jones) perched on the
very settle, every panel
blazoned with languishing
Pre-Raphaelite angels and
ladies. Here, the figure of Love
(Amor), holding a crescent
on which the supposed day
and hour of the death of
Dante's Beatrice are inscribed,
is flanked by the head of
Christ, in a striking Sunburst,
and the head of Beatrice,
set in the virginal Moon. The
whole expresses the view
that Love is the prime mover
of the Universe.

◁ **Annie Miller** *c.*1860

Pen and ink on paper

THE THEME OF THE 'gentleman' who marries 'beneath' him was common in Victorian literature – and the event not infrequent in Victorian life. Both Ford Madox Brown and Frederick Stephens married working-class women, and the austere Holman Hunt planned to do so. His choice was Annie Miller, his model. They were betrothed around the time of the dissolution of the PRB in 1853-54, but Hunt decided that marriage must wait until he had 'educated' her. He decreed that she must not model for other artists, especially Rossetti. The fickle Annie disobeyed and in 1857, when she confessed this to Hunt, the close friendship between the two artists ended. She perhaps confessed also to a sexual relationship with Rossetti, although her engagement to Hunt was not formally broken off until 1860. Annie was the model for a number of the sumptuous half-length portraits of Rossetti's 'Venetian period' (*c.*1859-69), notably *Helen of Troy* (1863), an embodiment of the *femme fatale* well suited to her disturbing beauty.

▷ **Miss Fanny Cornforth** 1860

Pencil on paper

IT IS NOT PRECISELY KNOWN when Rossetti met Fanny Cornforth (born Sarah Cox in 1824, and thus his senior by four years), who became one of his best models as well as his longest-lasting lover. She dated their meeting to 1856. She appears in the final version of *Found*, begun before that date, but was not the original model. Her first appearance in a definitely dated work is in the aptly titled *Bocca Baciata (Lips That Have Been Kissed)* of 1858-59. Fanny was the antithesis of tragic Elizabeth Siddal: a jolly, voluptuous cockney hoyden, nicknamed 'Helephant'. Her appeal was to Rossetti's earthy, sensual side, as the ideal relief from blessed damozels and striving for purity. Their on-off affair survived the dislike of many of Rossetti's friends, who accused her of stealing *objets d'art*, and their respective marriages in 1860. In 1863, with both spouses dead, she became titular housekeeper at Rossetti's home in Cheyne Walk, Chelsea. Their relationship did not end until she decided to marry again in 1879.

◁ **How They Met Themselves**
1851-60

Pen and ink and brush on paper

ROSSETTI COMPLETED this stark
and disturbing drawing while on
his honeymoon with Elizabeth
Siddal. The theme of the
Doppelgänger reflects the closeness
of the relationship – 'I am you;
you are me' – between Gabriel
and Elizabeth. Its expression, in
the depiction of the medieval
lovers horrified to meet their
doubles in the dark forest,
perhaps suggests the oppressive
quality, for both partners, of that
closeness. It may also manifest
Rossetti's increasing fears for
Elizabeth's health, for in legend
to meet one's double portends
death. Many of the portrayals
of Elizabeth by Gabriel express
their two-in-one partnership. He
shows her gazing into mirrors
being painted by him and even
paints her painting him. His
sister Christina summed up the
extent of his obsessive love for
Elizabeth in the first and last
lines of her sonnet *In an Artist's
Studio* (1856):

One face looks out
        from all his canvases
...Not as she is,
        but as she fills his dream.

▷ **Beata Beatrix** *c.*1862-70

Oil on canvas

As Elizabeth Siddal Rossetti's
precarious health worsened,
especially after the delivery of
a stillborn child in May 1861,
so her dependence on laudanum,
an addictive, opium-based
soporific, grew. On the evening
of 10 February, 1862, Rossetti
discovered her unconscious
from an overdose. She died
next morning; an inquest
found her death accidental.
Desolated, Rossetti buried his
manuscript poems with her
(later they were exhumed) –
and set out to commemorate
her death in one of his finest
paintings, a wholly successful
essay in rich, sombre colour.
Elizabeth is shown as Beatrice
in spiritual – and, one must
suggest, near-sexual – ecstasy at
the moment of her death,
marked on the sundial. The
white dove of the Annunciation,
transformed into a crimson
bird of death, brings to her lap
a white poppy, emblem of
sleep – and source of opium.
In the background the figures
of Love and Dante regard each
other against a view of
medieval Florence.

◁ **The Annunciation** 1861

Watercolour

IN JANUARY 1861 Rossetti joined William Morris, Burne-Jones, Ford Madox Brown and others in founding 'The Firm' (originally Morris, Marshall, Faulkner & Co. and later simply Morris & Co.), a limited company with grandiose plans for the production of furniture, stained glass, jewellery, embroidery and metalwork by artist-craftsmen. In his work for the Firm, Rossetti was able to give full range to his genius for decorative design. This glowing watercolour shows the Blessed Virgin receiving the message of the Archangel Gabriel (very much a Rossetti 'stunner') in a rose garden, a very different composition in both setting and mood from '*Ecce Ancilla Domini!*' (page 12). It is a preliminary study for two oil panels on the pulpit of St Mark's Church, Scarborough, a Gothic Revival edifice designed by Rossetti's close friend the architect George Frederick Bodley (1827-1907), who commissioned the work.

Algernon Charles Swinburne 1861

Watercolour on paper

◁ *Previous page 41*

THE LITERARY REPUTATION of Algernon Charles Swinburne (1837-1909) has endured less well than legends of his scandalous life. His name and notoriety were ensured by *Poems and Ballads* (1866). His verses, described by Ruskin as 'All hot like pies with the Devil's fingers in them', enthralled and shocked Victorian readers. The tiny, red-headed, demonically excitable poet was not the ideal person to calm Rossetti's emotional turmoil following Elizabeth Siddal's death. Nor was Swinburne's acolyte, the artist Simeon Solomon (1840-1905), alcoholic, drug-addict and homosexual. Both shared Rossetti's taste for erotica and scatological humour. The nature of some frolics enjoyed during their sojourns at Cheyne Walk may be guessed from Swinburne's reported invention of such parlour games as 'Piss in the Corner' and 'Bugger My Neighbour'. Taken in hand in 1879 by Theodore Watts-Dunton (1832-1914), Rossetti's friend and legal adviser, Swinburne reformed – at the cost of his genius. Solomon ended his life as a pauper in a workhouse.

▷ Girl at a Lattice 1862

Oil on canvas

THE MODEL FOR THIS decorative composition in Rossetti's 'Venetian style' was a maidservant employed by Ford Madox Brown. Although her wistful mouth and drooping eyelids seem to echo the features of the recently deceased Elizabeth Siddal, the nervous intensity of Rossetti's earlier works gives way here to open celebration of feminine charm. The ewer holding flowers on the sill may well have formed part of Rossetti's own collection of blue-and-white oriental ware. A passion for collecting Chinese porcelain and Japanese woodblock prints swept Parisian artistic circles from about 1860. Rossetti and his friend Whistler, who also featured blue-and-white ware in a number of his works of the 1860s, took the lead in introducing 'Chinamania' to Britain.

▷ **Joan of Arc Kissing the Sword of Deliverance** *c.*1863

Oil on canvas

THE INCREASE IN RICHNESS of Rossetti's colours in the 1860s may owe much to his experience of designing stained glass and other decorative projects for the Firm. In *Joan of Arc*, he united the rich colour and luxurious modelling of his 'Venetian period' with the idealism of earlier works. As a subject, Joan also had the appeal of a 'woman of power', like such other of his leading ladies as Lucrezia Borgia (page 15), Lilith and Astarte Syriaca (page 75). He made several versions of this work, including two watercolours in 1864 and an oil in 1882. The warrior saint, armoured beneath her robe, grasps the heavy sword with a formidable sense of purpose. William Rossetti named a Mrs Beyer as the model, but it has been suggested that the sitter was Aggie Manetti ('Fatty Aggie'), whom William described as having a profile with 'some analogy to that of the great Napoleon'.

◁ **The First Madness
of Ophelia** 1864

Watercolour

THE CHARACTER OF Shakespeare's
tragic Ophelia, driven mad by
Hamlet's rejection of her love
and his killing of her father,
had special resonance for
Rossetti. At the time that
Elizabeth Siddal first sat for
him, the very beginning of his
passion for her, she posed also
for Millais' *Ophelia* (1851-52).
Rossetti made a number of
sketches of Elizabeth as
Ophelia, and in *c.*1856 she
herself wrote a poem, *A Year
and a Day*, in which she
identified herself with the
drowning Ophelia, whose
destiny is '...a sadder dream/
When this sad dream is dead'.
After Elizabeth's death,
Rossetti worked up certain
of these sketches into
watercolours. The one shown
here portrays an incident that
does not occur in the play,
although it is likely enough:
Ophelia, having burst in on
the court in the first flush of
her madness, is led away from
the perturbed Claudius and
Gertrude by Horatio.

Venus Verticordia 1864–68

Oil on canvas

◁ *Previous page 47*

EARLY IN HIS CAREER, Rossetti resolved to avoid 'Ettyism'. The reference was to William Etty (1787-1849), famous for female nudes – often with artfully shadowed pubic regions – that escaped censure only because of the obvious innocence of the artist himself. For this reason, and perhaps because many of his patrons were conventionally minded businessmen rather than aesthetes, few of Rossetti's finished works include nude figures, although he made many preparatory life studies. *Venus Verticordia,* for which the model was a statuesque cook employed by a friend, is among the exceptions. Although the painting is a simple 'stunner', with little or no emotional sub-text, it was condemned by Ruskin for 'coarseness' – not of the female figure, but of the flowers! He was probably more disturbed by the image of a woman dominant through her beauty, at a time when agitation for women's rights was growing, than by the blossoms. As a friend of the artist remarked, 'I never heard a word breathed against the perfect respectability of a honeysuckle.'

▷ **The Merciless Lady** 1865

Watercolour

AROUND THE MID-1860s, Rossetti made several efforts to produce paintings imbued with the poetic idealism that characterizes many of his earlier works. This watercolour, echoing the style of his Arthurian period, was one of the results. Pleasant as it is, it cannot be said to fulfil Rossetti's aim. In the portrayal of the pathetic plight of a dark-haired maiden who cannot distract her lover's attention from a blonde charmer with a zither, sentiment triumphs over subject. Truth to life and moral seriousness are notably lacking. The theme is obscure; perhaps Rossetti alludes in the work's title to Keats's poem *La Belle Dame sans Merci,* which tells of a chance-met lady whose magical songs cause a knight to forget his true love. Deserted at last by the *femme fatale,* he is left to wander forlornly in a barren landscape where 'no birds sing'.

Detail

▷ **The Beloved (The Bride)** 1865-66

Oil on canvas

'MY BELOVED IS MINE and I am his, Let him kiss me with the kisses of his mouth....' Verses from the *Song of Solomon* and *Psalms* on its frame mark this as a biblical subject, but its effect is secular and sensual. The bride's unveiling makes plain her desire for the bridegroom. The theme of the blossom opening to the light, the woman opening to her lover, informs the composition. The boy (a girl in preliminary studies) in the foreground holds a vase of bridal roses, the attendants' faces frame that of the bride like the petals of a rose and floral motifs persist in the bride's rose-shaped ring, her head ornament and the pattern of her robe. Rossetti may have borrowed the idea of the page whose dark skin emphasizes the bride's lovely pallor from the *Olympia* of Manet, whom he had visited in Paris in 1864. A professional model, Marie Ford, sat for the bride. Keomi, gypsy mistress of the Pre-Raphaelite associate Frederick Sandys (*c.*1829-1904), modelled the handmaiden to the right.

△ **Christina Rossetti** *c.*1866

Coloured chalk on paper

ROSSETTI'S DRAWING of his sister Christina at the age of about 35 captures her intellectuality and austerity, and faithfully records the fading of the beauty that characterized her as a young woman. Closely associated with the PRB from its beginnings and a contributor (as 'Ellen Alleyne') to its short-lived journal *The Germ*, she was betrothed to a founder-member James Collinson. Unhappily, when Christina, a most devout High Anglican, discovered that Collinson had returned to Roman Catholicism, she broke off the engagement. It was, said William Rossetti, 'a blow from which she did not fully recover'. Some modern biographers have portrayed her as a repressed, hysterical spinster, reading into her poetry sexual symbolism that is surely unintended if it is, indeed, present. Her best lyrics place her among the major Victorian poets and her narrative pieces, *Goblin Market* (1862) and *The Prince's Progress* (1866), inspired some of her brother's finest illustrations.

▷ **Monna Vanna** 1866

Oil on canvas

ROSSETTI CONSIDERED THIS ebullient portrait to be one of his finest achievements. It is certainly the most overtly 'Venetian' work of his eponymous style, but critics are divided as to its merits. It has been described as cold and calculated, as an unfortunate attempt at aping fashionable portraiture of the time and even as 'a strong contender for being the nineteenth century's nastiest painting' (*The Pre-Raphaelites*; Timothy Hilton). Rossetti's 'Monna (Madonna) Vanna' seems to have nothing to do with the character of that name in the works of Dante and Boccaccio. The 'fickle ...self-centred character' discerned in *The Lady with the Fan* (an alternative title) by Frederick Stephens may owe something to the nature of the model. She was Alexa (Alice) Wilding, a dressmaker whom Rossetti reportedly picked up in the street. She so took his fancy that for some time he paid her a retainer to model for him alone.

◁ **Sibylla Palmifera** 1866-70

Oil on canvas

ALEXA WILDING is painted in a manner far removed from *Monna Vanna* (page 53) in what may arguably be considered the most appealing and satisfying, in its restraint of both mood and colour, of Rossetti's 'stunners'. It portrays the 'Soul's Beauty', the title given by Rossetti to the sonnet (Number LXXVII in his sequence *The House of Life*) he wrote to accompany it:

*Under the arch of Life, where love
    and death,
Terror and mystery, guard her
    shrine, I saw
Beauty enthroned....*

Around the Lady Beauty flit butterflies, emblematic of the soul; she holds the palm of victory in her right hand. As a companion piece, Rossetti painted *Lady Lilith*, portraying the 'Body's Beauty' in the person of the sensual demon who, in Jewish legend, was Adam's first wife. Fanny Cornforth sat for the original version, completed in 1868, but in 1872-73 Rossetti repainted it with the head of Alexa Wilding.

Ellen Smith 1867

Coloured chalk

▷ *Overleaf page 56*

ELLEN SMITH, who sat for the bridesmaid to the left in *The Beloved* (page 51) and was the subject of one of Rossetti's finest drawings in the *Study for 'Washing Hands'* (1865), was another of the painter's chance-met, working-class models. We are told that she worked 'as a laundry maid in a place close by [Cheyne Walk]'. She shares the attributes of his other 'stunners': a sensual mouth, a strong, well-modelled chin, large, soulful eyes and luxuriant hair. The year of this drawing saw the beginning of the physical problems that were to shadow Rossetti's later life. He began to have trouble with his eyes and, ever prone to neurosis and self-dramatization, expressed fears that he might lose his sight.

Mrs William J. Stillman 1869

Coloured chalk on paper

◁ *Previous page 57*

MARIA SPARTALI STILLMAN (1844-1927), an accomplished artist who studied under Ford Madox Brown, sat for several of Rossetti's later works. His *Mnemosyne* (1881) was inspired by a photograph of Maria in that role, taken by the pioneer portrait photographer Julia Margaret Cameron (1815-79). Although this drawing shows her as a conventional 'stunner', Rossetti complained: 'I find her head about the most difficult I ever drew. It depends not nearly so much on real form as on a subtle charm of life which one cannot re-create.' Maria's husband, the American art critic William James Stillman, was co-founder of the influential American art magazine *The Crayon*, which favourably noticed the Pre-Raphaelites when some of their works were shown in New York in 1857. It was Stillman who, around 1870, recommended Rossetti to take chloral, the drug to which he became addicted, for his insomnia.

▷ **Reverie** 1868

Coloured chalk on paper

IN 1857, WHILE WORKING on the Oxford Union murals, Rossetti and William Morris met 18-year-old Jane Burden, daughter of an ostler. It is probable that both fell in love with this girl who embodied the Pre-Raphaelite ideal of beauty, but because of Rossetti's commitment to Elizabeth Siddal, Morris took the prize, marrying Jane in 1859. After 1865, when financial difficulties forced Morris to give up his craft centre at the Red House, Bexley Heath, Kent, and move to London, Jane modelled regularly for Rossetti. The exact nature of their relationship remains a fruitful source of discussion, but it is certain that she exerted a major influence on both his later life and art. Photographs of Jane Morris, like the one taken at Cheyne Walk in 1865 from which this study was made, show that Rossetti did not exaggerate her beauty.

▷ **Pandora** 1869

Coloured chalk on paper

THIS STUDY IS one of the earliest of a series of works, ranging from drawings to oils, in which, over the best part of a decade (*c.*1869-79), Rossetti portrayed Jane Morris as Pandora. In Ancient Greek myth, Pandora ('All-Gifted') was the first woman made by Zeus, who gave to her a box that she was ordered to present, unopened, to the man she married. When Pandora or, according to some readings of the myth, her bridegroom opened the box, all the evils that have since troubled humankind flew out of it. Only one quality remained, Hope; and in some versions of Rossetti's picture Pandora's box carries the inscription *Ultima Manet Spes* ('Hope remains at last' It is suggested that the artist saw Jane Morris both as the 'all-gifted' woman and as the symbol of his remaining hopes for his life and his art.

▷ **Mrs Jane Morris Reclining on a Sofa** 1870

Pen and ink on paper

WHETHER ROSSETTI ENJOYED a sexual relationship with Jane Morris, there is no doubt that he loved her and that his love was in some measure returned. Some read meaning into the fact that Morris's only completed oil painting portrays Jane as *Queen Guinevere* (1858) and that he also showed her as *La Belle Iseult* – both women are among the great adulteresses of literature. This drawing was made in 1869, possibly while Rossetti and Jane were staying together at a cottage at Scalands, Sussex. William Morris was sometimes present, but does not seem to have been unwilling to leave them alone together. The American novelist Henry James, who visited Rossetti and the Morrises at this time, described Jane lying on the sofa: '...this dark silent medieval woman', adding, with his habitual feline touch, 'with her medieval toothache'. He did, however, praise her 'great wavy projections' of hair, and her 'strange, sad, deep, dark Swinburnian eyes'.

29 Nov
1870

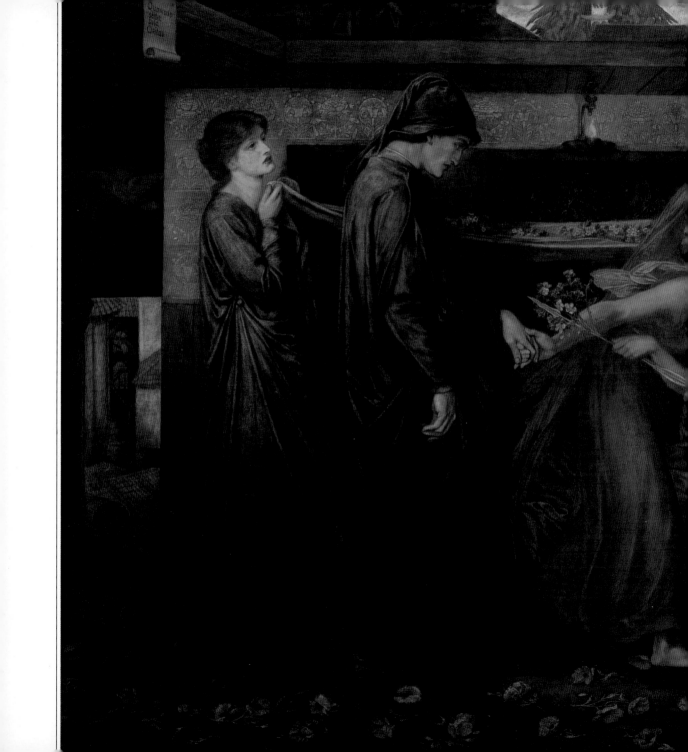

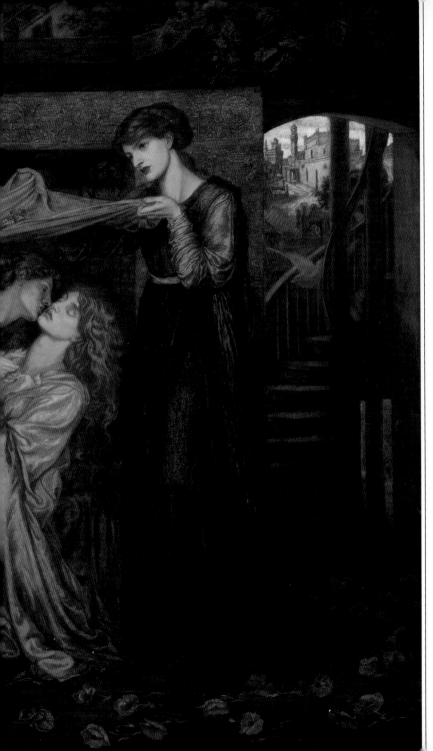

◁ **Dante's Dream at the Time of the Death of Beatrice** 1871

Oil on canvas

THE LARGEST OF ROSSETTI's oil paintings (211 x 317.5cm/83 x 125in) and last of his major works on themes from Dante demonstrates his mastery of the oil medium. The scene is taken from the *Vita Nuova*: Dante is led forward by Love, who wears the pilgrim's scallop shell, to look on the body of Beatrice as her attendants prepare to shroud it in a white pall strewn with hawthorn blossom. Echoing *Beata Beatrix* (page 39), poppies cover the floor and crimson doves come as messengers of death. The work was based on a watercolour of 1856, in which Elizabeth Siddal was shown as Beatrice. Here, Beatrice is Jane Morris and until repainting in 1881 had her dark hair. The attendants are Alexa Wilding (left) and Maria Stillman (right). Love has the features of Johnston Forbes-Robertson (1853-1937), later a famous actor-manager, while the face of Dante is that of Charles Augustus Howell, Rossetti's equivocal business agent.

Detail

▷ **The Blessed Damozel** 1871-78

Oil on canvas

ROSSETTI OFTEN WROTE POEMS to accompany his paintings but only once, with *The Blessed Damozel*, did the poem precede the painting. The poem was written in 1847 and the painting was commissioned by Rossetti's patron William Graham in 1871. The composition most happily captures the lyricism of the poem. The Damozel (Alexa Wilding)

'...leaned out from the gold bar of Heaven ...She had three lilies in her hand/And the stars in her hair were seven.' Below are palm-bearing angels and above, tenderly embracing lovers (angels in a second version, painted concurrently). The predella, showing her lover on Earth looking up to the transfigured beauty, was

added at Graham's request in 1878. Rossetti thought this 'one of my very best', but Theodore Watts-Dunton said it showed 'the difficulty of rendering by painting subjects that are specially adapted to be rendered by poetry' – a criticism that might more fairly be levelled at certain of Rossetti's other works.

▷ **Afternoon at Home** 1922
Louis Wain (1860–1939)

Gouache on paper

DESPITE BEING THE SECOND
President of the British
National Cat Club, the artist
Louis Wain chose always to
draw the cat as a cartoon
figure, clothed and semi-human
– a caricature of the real,
naturally dignified animal.
Wain's popularity as a cat
artist, at its height at the turn
of the century, grew out of the
postcard craze of the day. He
had been producing illustrations
for books published by Raphael
Tuck, who also published
postcards, and from 1902
Wain's cat pictures began
appearing on postcards. Soon
he was 'Catland's' most famous
artist. When the postcard
craze died out, Wain returned
to book illustration, producing
many children's cat books
for the well-known publisher,
Dean, among others.
Towards the end of his life,
when the schizophrenia
which had long threatened
him became inescapable,
the cats he continued
to draw in great numbers
became extraordinary
creatures indeed.

▷ **May Morris** 1872

Coloured chalk on paper

IN 1871 ROSSETTI and William
Morris took a joint tenancy on
Kelmscott Manor, Oxfordshire.
Rossetti was often alone there
with Jane and her two daughters,
Jenny and May. This portrait
of May, the younger, made
when she was ten years old,
shows the girl as a near double
of her mother. In character,
however, she proved more
like her father, sharing his
dedication to Socialism
and craftsmanship. An expert
needlewoman, in 1885 she
took over the management of
Morris & Company's embroidery
department. The delicacy and
tranquillity of this portrait
do not reflect Rossetti's mood
at the time of its making.
Infuriated in late 1871 by
an attack by the critic Robert
Buchanan on 'The Fleshly
School of Poetry', aimed
chiefly at Swinburne and
himself, he showed increasing
signs of paranoia. In June 1872
he broke down completely,
and attempted suicide by
taking laudanum (the fatal drug
taken by Elizabeth Siddal).

Detail

▷ **The Bower Meadow** 1872

Oil on canvas

'A BEAUTIFUL ROMANTIC DREAM, of something that never was, never will be....' Although these words were applied by Burne-Jones to his own work, they are equally apt for this fanciful composition. It has been denounced as a cynical exercise in which the artist, urgently needing money, took a landscape painted at Knole Park, Sevenoaks, Kent, as early as 1850, added a few romantic medieval-style figures, and found a ready market. Like his earlier 'musical fantasies', such as *The Blue Closet* (page 24) and *The Tune of the Seven Towers* (page 31), the subject has little meaning: two self-absorbed 'stunners' – Alexa Wilding (right) and Maria Stillman (left) – strum on psaltery and zither, while barefoot maidens caper languidly to their music. It its the ideal of beauty that Rossetti wished to convey, but lacks the poetic mystery of his more clearly defined subject pictures.

▷ **La Ghirlandata** 1873

Oil on canvas

THIS PROVIDES a further example of Rossetti's successful return to major work in oils, despite his worsening physical and mental condition, during the years 1871-74, when he lived with William and Jane Morris at Kelmscott Manor. Alexa Wilding went there to model for this painting, in which the features of the angels are those of May Morris. Rich colours, with strikingly contrasted greens, enhanced by the skilful use of glazing, a technique in which Rossetti excelled, make *La Ghirlandata* one of the best of what may be described as his 'art for art's sake' pictures. It was purchased by one of the artist's most important patrons, the Liverpool shipping magnate Frederick Richard Leyland. He thought so highly of Rossetti that he bought 12 of his oils and 26 of his drawings to hang alongside paintings by such Renaissance masters as Botticelli, Filippo Lippi and Giorgione.

◁ **Proserpine** 1877

Oil on canvas

IN ROMAN LEGEND Proserpine
was kidnapped and forced into
marriage by Pluto, ruler of the
underworld. Jupiter decreed
that she could be freed, provid-
ed she had not eaten any fruits
of Hades. Because she had
eaten a single pomegranate
seed, she was condemned to
spend half of each year in the
underworld. Rossetti shows
Jane Morris as the unhappy
girl, holding the disastrous
pomegranate, the darkness of
her subterranean life briefly
illuminated by a gleam of light
from the world above that
touches an ivy strand symbolizing
memory. Although the subject
may have been suggested by
Swinburne's 'Proserpina' poems
(Rossetti's own 'Proserpine',
in Italian, is seen at top left),
it obviously had great resonance
for him: he embarked on
no fewer than eight versions
(most unfinished) of the
painting. It is generally accepted
that he intended a reference
to his belief that Jane Morris
was tied to a husband she
did not love.

▷ **Astarte Syriaca** 1877

Oil on canvas

JANE MORRIS APPEARS as yet another *femme fatale* in the shape of the Syrian goddess of love, manifesting, as an early commentator on Rossetti remarked, 'lurid and terrible royalty...she reigns in a dark serenity which nothing can appal'. It is certainly not a comfortable image of love: this is a woman who fully realizes, even relishes, her sexual power over men. Jane Morris, having recently discovered the full extent of Rossetti's drug addiction, may have been threatening to break off their relationship at this time. In a sonnet written to accompany the work, Rossetti described Astarte's 'love-freighted lips and absolute eyes', a reference to his often expressed belief that the mouth reflected the sensual nature of love and the eyes its spiritual aspect. The glowing, glazed greens, not uncommon in Rossetti's later works, echo the Veronese-inspired paintings of his 'Venetian' period.

◁ **Santa Lilias** 1879

Coloured chalk

THE 'CHRISTIAN NATURALISM' of the Pre-Raphaelite Brotherhood was far in the past when Rossetti made this drawing of a 'stunner' in a sacred setting. Note how the sinuous draperies, the mannered hands and the staging of the composition anticipate the Art Nouveau style which Rossetti's later work greatly influenced. Despite his idealism, Rossetti was always an acute businessman and when his patrons demanded 'stunners' he was happy enough to supply them—while privately scoffing at the 'Lilliputian leanings' of the buyers. It is easy to criticize the artist for the apparent commercialism of some of his later compositions. It must be remembered that neither his physical nor his mental state was conducive to sustained effort. Indeed, it is surprising that so many of the paintings executed after *c.*1870 rank among his best.

▷ **The Lady of Pity** *c.*1879

Oil on canvas

THIS PAINTING, among the most
appealing – as among the least
feverish – of Rossetti's portraits
of Jane Morris, is one of the
alternative versions of the oil
La Donna della Finestra (1879).
The subject is taken from
Dante's Vita Nuova: a lady
looks down from her window
on the poet, pitying his grief
as he laments the death of
Beatrice. On the sill before
her lie the ivy leaves of
remembrance; in a scroll
below her is the inscription:
color d'amore e di pietá sembiante
('the colour of love and
appearance of pity'). It is
interesting to compare the
treatment of Jane Morris's
beauty here with that of
Day Dream (page 78). Here,
her loveliness manifests itself
in spirituality; there, in sexual
allure. But, as in the case of
Elizabeth Siddal, knowledge
of whether Rossetti's
relationship with Jane was
consummated sexually matters
little to our understanding of
the works she inspired.

▷ **Day Dream** 1880

Oil on canvas

AFTER DISCOVERING the extent
of his drug addiction in *c.*1877,
Jane Morris had ceased
regularly to meet or model
for Rossetti, although they
kept up an affectionate
correspondence. 'I left off
going to him on account of
the children...', she later
explained. This major oil was
based on a pastel and chalk
drawing made at Kelmscott
Manor in 1878, showing Jane
sitting in a tree. He made
many studies of a sycamore
tree in his garden at Cheyne
Walk in preparation for this
lovely image of Jane. She
seems, in her voluptuous
reverie, to be herself a force
of nature: one feels that it is
by the power of her creative
dream that the buds of
the tree unfold. In the
original drawing, she held a
convolvulus flower on her
open book. Here, it is
changed to a honeysuckle
blossom, whose rich scent and
clutching, tongue-shaped
petals suggest sexuality.

ACKNOWLEDGEMENTS

The publisher would like to thank the Bridgeman Art Library, London for their help in researching and supplying transparencies for pictures illustrated in this book.

The Bridgeman Art Library, London/Private Collection – 9, 14; /**The Tate Gallery, London** – 11 (detail p.10), 12, 24, 27, 28, 29, 50 (detail p.51), 74; /**Manchester City Art Galleries** – 17, 71 (detail p.70), 75; /**Delaware Art Museum, Wilmington, USA** – 19 (detail p.18); /**Christie's, London** – 20-1, 45, 59, 69; /**Fitzwilliam Museum, University of Cambridge** – 25, 33 (detail p.32), 37, 38, 40, 41, 43, 52; /**British Museum, London** – 34; /**The Fine Art Society, London** – 36, 49; /**Oldham Art Gallery, Lancs** – 46; /**Russell-Cotes Art Gallery and Museum, Bournemouth** – 47; /**Victoria and Albert Museum, London** – 56, 78; /**The Maas Gallery, London** – 57; /**The Paringdon Collection, Buscot, Oxon** – 61; / **Phillips Fine Art Auctioneers, London** – 62-3, 76; /**Lady Lever Art Gallery, Port Sunlight, Birmingham** – 67 (detail p.66); **Guidhall Art Gallery, Corporation of London** – 73; /**Bradford City Art Galleries and Museums** – 77;

The Tate Gallery, London – 22-3, 53

The Board of Trustees of the National Museums and Galleries of Merseyside/The Walker Art Gallery, Liverpool – 64-5; /**The Lady Lever Art Gallery, Port Sunlight, Birmingham** – 54.

We apologise in advance for any unintentional error in attributing acknowledgement. We would be pleased to insert the appropriate acknowledgement in any subsequent edition of this publication should the occasion arise.